Philosophy of Religion

AS Revision Guide AQA Unit C

Brian Poxon and Charlotte Davidson

First published 2014

by PushMe Press

Mid Somerset House, Southover, Wells, Somerset BA5 1UH

www.pushmepress.com

© 2014 Inducit Learning Ltd

British Library Cataloguing in Publication Data
A catalogue record for this book is available from the British Library

ISBN: 978-1-909618-98-5 (pbk)
ISBN: 978-1-78484-023-5 (hbk)
ISBN: 978-1-78484-021-1 (ebk)
ISBN: 978-1-78484-022-8 (pdf)

Typeset in Frutiger by booksellerate.com
Printed by Lightning Source

A rich & engaging community assisted by the best teachers in Philosophy

philosophy.pushmepress.com

Students and teachers explore Philosophy of Religion through handouts, film clips, presentations, case studies, extracts, games and academic articles.

Pitched just right, and so much more than a textbook, here is a place to engage with critical reflection whatever your level. Marked student essays are also posted.

Contents

The Cosmological Argument

KEY TERMS

- **A POSTERIORI** - Knowledge gained after experience.

- **COSMOLOGICAL ARGUMENT** - Reasoning concerning the origins, nature and order of the cosmos.

- **CONTINGENT EXISTENCE** - Something which, by its nature, does not necessarily have to exist, and could or could not have existence, eg you or me. Once existent, can go out of existence.

- **DEDUCTION** - A type of reasoning whereby it is demonstrated that the conclusion necessarily follows from the premises (as seen in the ontological argument).

- **INDUCTION** - A type of reasoning that takes specific instances and from them, draws a general conclusion (eg as seen in the cosmological argument).

- **INFINITE REGRESS** - In the cosmological argument, this refers to a chain of causes going back that has no beginning.

- **NECESSARY BEING** - A being whose non-existence is a contradiction.

- **PHENOMENAL** - Things which are perceived by the senses or by immediate experience.

AQUINAS'S COSMOLOGICAL ARGUMENT

The cosmological argument stands in contrast to the OA in that it is not deductive but **INDUCTIVE**. Aquinas put forward five ways for the existence of God, and the cosmological argument (CA) was outlined in the first three of those ways; Aquinas argued for the existence of God from **MOTION, CAUSE** and **NECESSITY**.

Aquinas commenced his argument with the **A POSTERIORI** evidence of the universe itself and asked why it existed (not just why there are things within the universe, but why there is a universe at all). Upon analysing such evidence, Aquinas noted that some things are in motion. By motion, Aquinas meant the change that goes on in particular things within the universe, such as within a tree as it grows taller or sheds bark. (Note here that for Aquinas, following Aristotle, motion did not just mean physical movement, as something could be still and yet be changing, like the aforementioned tree.)

For something to be in motion it must be, in Aquinas's words, **"MOVED BY ANOTHER"** (something external to it). He gave an example of wood, which is changed/acted upon by fire to reach its potential of becoming hot. The change, Aquinas noted, could not be caused by the thing itself; something acted/moved to make the wood hot (fire), but then something moved to make the fire (friction) and so on.

Aquinas considered the possibility of this chain of motion going backwards infinitely (infinite regress) to get to an ultimate explanation for motion, but noted that this was not possible.

> *There would then be no first mover, and, consequently, no subsequent mover, as subsequent movers move only insofar as they are moved by the first mover. - Aquinas*

Aquinas, working from Aristotle, understood this first or prime, unmoved mover to be God.

Aquinas's second way is his argument from **FIRST CAUSE**. Nothing is its own efficient cause as it would "have to exist prior to itself", which is impossible. Again, it is not possible to go back infinitely in the chain of causes as without a first cause there would be no subsequent intermediate causes which would mean that there would be no present effects (things we see in place around us now). "Plainly this is not the case," noted Aquinas, "so we must admit a first efficient cause (itself uncaused) which everyone calls 'God'."

Aquinas's third way is based upon the idea of **NECESSITY** and **CONTINGENCY**. Contingent things are those things which could or could not be in existence; they are non-permanent - if they come into being, they go out of being. Because of that, "it is impossible for them always to exist, for that which is possible not to be at some time does not exist. If everything is like that, at one time nothing existed.* If that were true, there would be nothing in existence now, because things only come to exist because of things already existing."

Thus Aquinas posits the need for a necessary being whose necessity lies in itself because if everything was only contingent then there would be nothing today.

If there was a state of nothingness then **EX NIHILO NIHIL FIT**, (out of nothing, nothing comes), and yet there is something - so there must be something that has necessary existence. Things do not have to exist, but they do, and this could not be the case if everything was entirely contingent. The required necessary being is God, unmoved mover and first cause.

COPLESTON'S COSMOLOGICAL ARGUMENT AND RUSSELL'S RESPONSE

In 1948, a famous debate between **COPLESTON** and **RUSSELL** outlined key differences in understandings of any ultimate explanation for the universe. Copleston's argument from **CONTINGENCY** relied on the argument from Liebniz's **PRINCIPLE OF SUFFICIENT REASON**. Liebniz asked why there is something rather than nothing, which led him to look for an ultimate reason for the existence of the universe. He argued that there needs to be "sufficient reason" to explain why something is the case. With regard to the existence of the universe, this sufficient reason cannot be given from the collection or sum of its constituent parts, as these are insufficient to explain the whole thing. The sufficient reason must be external to the universe because contingent things don't explain their own existence but are reliant on other contingent things.

This principle, and the way in which it is disputed, is central to the Copleston and Russell debate. In summary, the argument went as follows:

- Copleston put forward the need for a **PRINCIPLE OF SUFFICIENT REASON** that is not found within the collection of contingent beings within the universe.

- Russell asked for clarification of such a principle, and wanted to know when precisely a sufficient reason is reached, and if sufficient reason for existence is the same as **CAUSE**.

Copleston noted that we can attribute cause to things that are contingent but that sufficient reason refers to a total explanation as to how the universe as a whole is in existence, not just those contingent things within it, which rely on being caused.

He stressed the inability of contingent things to provide their own sufficient reason; the reason for their existence must lie outside of them. If God is another contingent being, then he cannot have within him the complete reason for his own existence.

AS A NECESSARY (NOT CONTINGENT) BEING, GOD IS HIS OWN SUFFICIENT CAUSE.

Russell questioned the need for a sufficient reason, and whether such was possible anyway. Is it possible to go from contingent causes within the universe to a necessary sufficient and external reason, and wondered how such a move would be possible. Russell also said that necessary only applied to **ANALYTIC** statements such as "a bachelor is an unmarried man", and saw no ground to talk of God as necessary.

Copleston responded by saying that just because a thing has not been found (the sufficient reason) it is not the same as saying it should not be looked for. The contingent cause of events cannot provide a sufficient reason for the whole series; hence the need for a necessary being.

Russell maintained that the world "just is"; it is **BRUTE FACT**. And that it is not possible to go from causes within the universe to a cause of the universe (famously saying that just because every human being has a mother, it does not mean the entire race has a mother). Here he is accusing Copleston of the **FALLACY OF COMPOSITION**, which assumes that what is true of parts must be true of the whole.

Copleston replied that God as a necessary being is not a first cause or mother as such, as that would mean God is another "phenomenal" and contingent cause, which would not explain the whole series. God is an **ONTOLOGICAL NECESSITY**.

HUME'S CRITICISMS OF THE COSMOLOGICAL ARGUMENT

Hume questioned why the world needs a first cause or a beginning. Why is infinite regress impossible? Even if we see cause and effect in the world (and Hume questioned this assumption), it does not mean that the universe itself be the effect of an uncaused cause, but the chain of causes could simply continue ad infinitum.

Furthermore, Hume famously challenged our understanding of cause and effect, noting that event a following event b does not meant that a caused b, even if we have not seen one instance when b did not happen after a. His argument noted that we put cause and effect together by habit rather than having any evidence that one caused the other. Hume's argument continues to carry much weight today and his questioning of cause has implications for Aquinas's claim that God is the first cause.

Hume questioned why there could not be more than one cause. The empirical evidence from the world gives no clues as to the number of causes that it required (if it required any), and, without being able to go outside the universe, Hume questioned how we would know if there was one or more causes. Maybe male and female Gods who are born and then die are more fitting from the empirical evidence we see in the world IF **EFFECTS RESEMBLE CAUSES** in any way – such Gods may fit the profile of the a posteriori evidence more closely than a Christian God. To stress, Hume, writing as an empiricist (and, remember, Aquinas is working from an a posteriori base), noted that we have no experience of the causer(s) of the universe, which seems to be a unique case; we have experience of what we have called cause and effect within the world but how can we know about a cause outside the world; on what experience would we base such?

Hume questioned if the uniting together of different things within the universe and saying that "the whole" has a cause is "**AN ARBITRARY ACT OF THE MIND**". There is nothing in our experience, or any logical argument that can be made, to suggest that there is an overarching cause which gives a reason for the effects we see in the universe.

In response, Elizabeth **ANSCOMBE** has questioned Hume's argument about not being able to say that existence has not got a cause because we cannot go outside the universe to know that. She writes that it is possible to conclude that "existence must have a cause" without knowing specifically "that particular effects must have particular causes". While it is possible to imagine things coming into existence without a cause, this does not tell us if this is the case in reality.

STRENGTHS

- **TRUE TO SCIENCE** - Could Aquinas's argument from causation actually tie together with scientific evidence of causation? Some scientists argue that Big Bang cosmology requires a causal factor. With the discovery of the Higgs Boson particle, the question still remains as to why such an important particle is in place. If we accept that we need to find an ultimate explanation or, as Leibniz stressed, a sufficient reason, do the arguments of Aquinas and Copleston still offer some useful ground?

- **WE DON'T NEED A CAUSE** - Is the discovery of effects without causes sufficient to fatally attack Aquinas's causation argument? Could it be that the cause of such effects has not yet been discovered rather than there not being a cause for them?

- **PROGRESS** - The progress of science would cease if we took Russell's line that "things just are". The developments we have seen are because we have attempted to answer the questions "Why are things the way they are? What is the explanation in this and that case?" Perhaps Copleston was actually being more scientific in his quest for an answer to the whole series of events.

WEAKNESSES

- **NEW DISCOVERIES** - In the field of Quantum Mechanics, research is being carried out as to the idea of "backward causation", and even the notion of uncaused events, and it is possible that our whole notion of what is meant by cause and effect will need to be re-evaluated. It may also be possible that matter or energy is eternal, and as such the necessary element of Aquinas's argument is not God but material itself. We can still ask, however, why that it is the case that matter has an eternal nature ("it just has" might be Russell's response, and this is an acceptable position for many).

- Aquinas was asking why there is **ANY MOVEMENT AT ALL**, rather than just proposing God as some kind of first pusher of a chain of events. For Aquinas, God is not the one who winds up the clockwork mouse and leaves it to run, but rather the one who is the necessary mover, the cause of all causes whose activity, unlike the one who winds up the mouse, has not ceased. God, for Aquinas, is the ultimate explanation for why there is cause or movement, the ultimate cause, without whom there is no ongoing universe, cause, movement or any contingent things.

- **NOTHING EXISTED** - It is perhaps not difficult to understand that a string of contingent beings could always be in existence, overlapping in the time that they have being. This would mean, contrary to Aquinas's argument, that there never was a time when nothing existed, even from a contingent basis. Alternatively, could there be things which have always been in existence but will go out of existence at some time in the future?

KEY QUOTES

1. *"The First-Cause argument rests on the assumption that every series must have a first term, which is false; for example, the series of proper fractions has no first term."* Russell

2. *"To say that such a very complex and well-ordered universe comes into being without any cause or reason is equivalent to throwing one's hands up in the air and just saying that anything at all might happen, that it is hardly worth bothering to look for reasons at all. And that is the death of science."* Ward

3. *"Though difficult, and still incomplete, there is no reason to believe that the greatest problem, how the universe came into being, and what it is, will not be solved; we can safely presume that the solution will be comprehensible to human minds. Moreover, that understanding will be achieved this side of the grave."* [ie the answer will be provided by science and not metaphysical reasoning or religion] Atkins

4. *"Not how the world is, but that it is, is the mystery."* Wittgenstein

CONFUSIONS TO AVOID

The easy reply to Aquinas which is often given, which runs along the lines of "if everything needs a cause, what caused God?" is perhaps not the strongest one to make, in that it does not understand what Aquinas regards as cause or what he is suggesting we should understand God to be. God is not "one other thing" or the first flicker of the line of dominoes, but the necessary unmoved cause on whom all other movement, change, cause and contingency is reliant.

Be very careful to understand and able to explain the **DIFFERENCES** between the cosmological arguments of Aquinas and Copleston; they are related but different, and the use of Liebniz's Principle of Sufficient Reason will help you in your delineation of these differences.

Religious Experience

KEY TERMS

- **CORPORATE RELIGIOUS EXPERIENCE** - Religious experience that happens to a number of people at the same time.

- **INEFFABLE** - Something that cannot be described in normal language.

- **NOETIC** - Knowledge revealed during a religious experience which is not available through other means such as study.

- **NON-PROPOSITIONAL REVELATION** - God reveals himself through the experience of the believer, accepted by faith.

- **NUMINOUS EXPERIENCE** - Awareness or direct experience of the presence of something "wholly other".

- **PASSIVITY** - The recipient is not in control and is being acted upon rather than initiating the experience themselves.

- **PRINCIPLE OF CREDULITY** - Unless we have good reasons to think otherwise we should accept that how things seem to be is how they are.

- **PRINCIPLE OF TESTIMONY** - Unless we have good reasons to think otherwise we should accept other people's testimony, including their account of their experiences.

- **PROPOSITIONAL REVELATION** - God reveals facts or truths about himself either through natural revelation or through Holy Scripture.

- **TRANSIENT** - A brief and temporary experience as far as time is concerned.

A **RELIGIOUS EXPERIENCE** is sometimes used as an **A POSTERIORI** argument for the existence of God and provides unique challenges to the philosopher of religion. Careful definition has to be in place, and rigorous **ANALYSIS** and **EVALUATION** have to be offered, using specific examples (eg visions and voices).

SWINBURNE classifies religious experiences into **PUBLIC** and **PRIVATE** categories, though **JACKSON** notes these are not always as clear-cut as this distinction suggests:

PUBLIC RELIGIOUS EXPERIENCES are:

a. Where people perceive the action of God through an ordinary event, for example, in the beauty of a sunset.

b. Those which are observable but unusual, such as Jesus walking on water or healing a leper, in which natural laws are violated.

PRIVATE RELIGIOUS EXPERIENCES:

a. Happen to a person who then describes them in ordinary language. For example, Moses' experience at the burning bush (Exodus 3) or an angel appearing to Joseph to announce the birth of Christ (Matthew 1:20).

b. Happen but cannot be explained to others, for example, mystical experiences such as those of Teresa of Ávila.

c. Involve someone becoming aware more generally of the presence of God, which is interpreted from a religious perspective.

Religious experiences can also be divided into **DIRECT** and **INDIRECT** experiences. Direct experiences refer to where a person feels that they directly encounter God or the Divine. This could be:

a. **SEEING A VISION** - Such as described by the young girl Bernadette at Lourdes.

b. **HEARING A VOICE** - Such as described by Samuel in the Old Testament. (1 Samuel 3:1-21)

c. **AN ENCOUNTER** - Or a distinct awareness of a presence. **OTTO** describes this as the **NUMINOUS** or "apprehension of the wholly other", suggesting that God is above knowledge and logic. Otto describes it as different to the mystical which seeks unity of all things; a numinous experience is mysterious, tremendum et fascinans - mysterious, awe-inspiring in an overwhelming and almost terrifying way, and fascinating. It draws us towards the divine.

DREAMS that are recorded in the Bible (for example, Jacob, Genesis 28: 10-22 or Peter, Acts 10:1-28) are times when a voice or vision is described as part of a direct experience. But what do we mean by "direct" and "encounter" when a person is asleep?

INDIRECT experiences are when a person is moved or inspired by nature or in prayer and/or worship to think of and reflect upon the Divine, which might lead to a response of submission, repentance, confession and/or thanksgiving. **KIRKWOOD** uses an analogy to describe the difference between direct and indirect religious experiences: Imagine a person arriving at their house to find a bear eating the porridge, (direct experience) as opposed to arriving after the event to find clues that a bear has been there, such as an empty bowl and droppings on the floor (indirect experience).

"Some people have suggested that indirect experiences are not necessarily different from ordinary experiences; they are made significant by the person who has the experience and for whom the experience has religious meaning." (**TAYLOR**) The acronym **PIE** raises an important point about whether a person's existing perspective affects what type of interpretation they give.

(**P**) A person's existing **PERSPECTIVE** affects their

(**I**) **INTERPRETATION OF THE EVENT**, which affects their

(**E**) understanding of the **EXPERIENCE**

Would you interpret a sunset as light from a massive ball of energy reflecting on water, (through natural laws governing light and reflection), or evidence of the beauty that God has placed within creation? Does this interpretation depend on your existing perspective on the question of God's existence? **JAMES** argued that some people are unlikely ever to have a religious experience because they would not be open to such an event being a possibility.

Sometimes a person's existing perspective is changed through a religious experience, particularly during a direct experience (in which case **PIE** would not be the model to apply). This was particularly the case in the story of **PAUL** when he was not looking for an encounter with Jesus, but was trying to stop people speaking about Christ being the Messiah. This is an example of a **CONVERSION EXPERIENCE**; a more recent example would be the conversion to Christianity of CS Lewis, author of The Lion, the Witch and the Wardrobe (and much more!).

A useful question to ask is if any change in the recipient of the experience is far more likely to happen during a direct as opposed to an indirect religious experience. The question of how much our existing perspective affects our experience, or whether such can be changed and overcome in a dramatic religious experience, is also worth pursuing in an essay, and it can open links to whether a religious experience is "simply" a psychological experience, (see James later) a "feeling" or a combination of these, and possibly more. Are all of the above experiences simply events which make people view the world in a different way when a person has reached a particular stage in life? They might be influenced by a specific occasion that then shapes their life and subsequent worldview and psychology. This does not mean necessarily that the event was a "religious" experience, but that the event was interpreted that way. **HICK** regards this as "experiencing as" - where two people will view the same event differently and such viewing will affect the way the event and the wider world is perceived.

Religious experiences may be both the strongest proof that God exists for a person who has had one, and the weakest argument for the onlooker, as it is difficult to assess the evidence second-hand. Keep in mind therefore the question of whether religious experiences are **VERIDICAL**, and, if so, how; can they be shown to be what the recipient believes them to be, that is, "experiences of God rather than delusions"? **(TAYLOR)**

THE VARIETIES OF RELIGIOUS EXPERIENCES (WILLIAM JAMES)

James found that there were four distinguishing features of a mystical religious experience:

- **PASSIVE** - The person who has this type of religious experience is not in control of what is happening; it is not willed by the person but they feel that they are in the grip of a superior power during it.

- **INEFFABLE** - It is not possible to describe the experience in normal language (see Swinburne's private experiences, point b above).

- **NOETIC** - The person receives some significant and authoritative knowledge and illumination, **REVEALED** through intuition rather than to the intellect, that could not be gained without this experience.

- **TRANSIENT** - The actual experience is short, (though sometimes time seems to be suspended for the recipient having the experience) but the effects of it are long-lasting.

As well as identifying what he felt was going on during a mystical experience, (which is an existential judgement) **JAMES** studied what such religious experiences meant for the recipient (which is a value judgement), and concluded that:

1. Religious experiences have a significant impact upon a person's life in that they:

    a. have great **AUTHORITY** for the person

b. are understood by the recipient to be **VERY REAL** (James was impressed by the **CERTAINTY** of the experiences he studied) and

c. can bring about real and **LONG-LASTING CHANGE** in the person's life. In fact, James said that the feelings of reality from a religious experience are more convincing than "results established by logic ever are", and that the results of the experience demonstrate that something of great value has taken place.

2. The view of the world, and our place within it, alters following the event; for example peacefulness, hope and love of others come more easily. The religious aims, following a person's conversion, become the "habitual centre of his energy". Whether induced or spontaneous, these experiences ("states of consciousness" - **JORDAN** et al) have long-lasting effects.

3. Religious experiences are part of a person's psyche, yet James concludes that there might be a supernatural element also. Neither was he concerned that they could be a product of neurosis, as **FREUD** would argue, suggesting that it was not necessary to have a "whole mind" to have a religious experience, marked by great certainty about the event. "For James, saying that religious experiences are psychological phenomena is a statement that a religious experience is natural to a person, just like other psychological experiences such as self-awareness or thinking." (**TAYLOR**) James takes an **EMPIRICAL** approach to religious experience, suggesting that these events "point with reasonable probability to the continuity of our consciousness with a wider, spiritual environment". (**JAMES**)

However, this does lead to the problem of whether a religious experience is just "real for them" and of no worth when used as an argument for a God who is objective, really "out there" (rather than in the mind).

What James was very careful to conclude was that the religious experiences he studied **DID NOT ACT AS PROOF FOR GOD** but that the individual had encountered what they perceived to be the Divine, the effects of which were very real. Religious experience "cannot be cited as unequivocally supporting the infinitist belief ... but that we can experience union with something larger than ourselves and in that union find our greatest peace". (**JAMES**)

Strengths

1. **OBJECTIVE** - James is someone trained in the medical profession studying similar experiences and effects experienced by a range of people. James is not out to prove the existence of God from his studies but to take an objective approach to what he finds.

2. **NOETIC** - We expect to find noetic elements if an encounter with a divine being has taken place. Whilst this leaves the onlooker no wiser as to what happened, it may be the case that description of it in ordinary language is not possible.

3. **EXPERIENTIAL** - James does not suggest that religious experiences bypass the human psyche, but includes emotions and feelings as part of the evidence for a religious experience.

Weaknesses

1. **TOO BROAD** - James's conclusions about religious experiences are so broad that religious experience could include drug-induced hallucinations. The lack of regard for how doctrine and creeds work to move the believer away from too much emphasis on subjective experience could be seen as a weakness in James's understanding of religion.

2. **PRE-DETERMINED** - If religious experiences are real it begs the question why people in different religions experience very different revelations. The doctrine of the religion seems to determine the type of experience (for example, the Cross and **STIGMATA**).

3. **LACK OF AUTHORITY -** James's conclusion that mystical religious experiences could be psychological in origin has been criticised, as, if this is the case, notes **MACKIE**, they lack any real authority, and are no different to other psychological experiences. However, God may have put that desire for him into people's psyche and therefore religious experiences are a natural part of personhood.

4. **ASSUMES REALISM** - James concluded that an undoubtedly real event has to be caused by a reality. Thus, God as a real being, could be the cause of the real event, if that is what a person believes. Is this a strong or valid argument?

SWINBURNE, in his analysis of a number of arguments for God, put forward two principles when assessing religious experiences:

1. The **PRINCIPLE OF CREDULITY** states that "if it seems to a subject that X is present, then probably X is present; what one seems to perceive probably is so".

   It is entirely up to the person who is listening to the account of the religious experience to prove that the person who had the experience did not do so; the burden of proof does not lie with the person who is describing the account.

2. The **PRINCIPLE OF TESTIMONY** states that people usually tell the truth. Swinburne argues that in everyday life, our default position is to believe that people have told us what they have actually perceived to have happened. The burden rests on the person who does not believe that we have told the truth to prove that is the case.

Swinburne recognises situations which would challenge the principle of credulity.

1. A person could be drunk or hallucinating or an unreliable witness.

2. Similar perceptions have been proved to be false.

3. It can be shown that whoever/whatever the recipient was claiming to have experienced was not actually present during the experience.

4. It is possible to show that "whatever/whoever the recipient is claiming to have experienced was there, but was not involved in/ responsible for the experience". (**JORDAN** et al)

The principle of testimony suggests that we should accept the statement about what has happened during a religious experience unless further proof is provided (as above) which suggests that the person is not telling the truth.

The most significant challenge relates to points 3 and 4. James has already suggested that the impairments suggested in point 1 need not necessarily bar a person from having a religious experience; however, how one disproves or proves that it was God involved in the religious experience seems a very great challenge as we are not talking here about the experience we have when we encounter another human being.

MACKIE also suggests that it is perfectly conceivable that a normally reliable person could be either mistaken or give a false account, and thus Swinburne's principle of testimony does not hold. The balance of probability "suggests that the mistake is more likely than the supernatural explanation, however sincere they might be" (in **AHLUWALIA**). Do the normal rules about how we recount sensory experiences apply in the case of religious experiences? **RUSSELL** also suggests that there are cases which meet Swinburne's criteria in which people have said that they have encountered Satan rather than God.

CORPORATE RELIGIOUS EXPERIENCE

A corporate religious experience is when many people seem to undergo the same experience and demonstrate similar responses, for example "All of the disciples were filled with the Holy Spirit and began to speak in other languages, as the Spirit gave them ability", **ACTS 2**. The annual Hajj pilgrimage by Muslims is another example of corporate religious experience.

THE TORONTO BLESSING (20 January 1994). Following a message to the Toronto Airport Church from visiting preacher Randy Clark, people began to laugh, cry, fall to the floor, roar like lions, speak in tongues and claim healings. The blessing spread to Christian churches around the world.

WILKINSON and **CAMPBELL** note that it would still be necessary to evaluate each person's experience as some might be carried along with the atmosphere, whilst others might fake an experience. Social psychologists also point to group hysteria.

What does Toronto show of a God who is love, which is a central Christian belief? Would all the events described above be consistent with existing belief? Does God take away human reason, and is it reasonable to think that God would visit "a small group in Toronto while doing nothing for the starving of Somalia or the persecuted [Christians] in China"? Wilkinson and Campbell have strayed into the dangerous territory of trying to guess the mind of God here, but critical analysis of corporate religious experiences is essential. We could apply the tests that James and Swinburne suggest to these unusual events.

RESPONSES TO THE IDEA OF RELIGIOUS EXPERIENCES

1. **COLE** - How is it possible to say that we have had an encounter with God if we have no previous knowledge of what God is? How could we recognise and identify the "other" as God? To say that the experience is one in which we "just know" it is God is philosophically dubious because, as **COLE** notes, it is based on a conviction rather than reasons.

2. **STARBUCK** - Carried out a study of **CONVERSION**, and noted that most religious conversions happen in late teens/early twenties when people speak of finding a peace through beginning to follow God. However, he found that, at that same stage in life, many non-religious young people also went through a stage of psychological angst and unease before finding their own identity in early adult life, and this process did not involve a religious conversion event. However, **EYRE** et al write that, in response to Starbuck, "some theists recognise that there are psychological aspects of conversion experiences but argue that to reduce conversion to just a psychological phenomenon fails to address the question of the cause of the experience".

3. **FREUD** - Argued that religious experiences are reactions to a hostile world, in which we seek help from a father figure. Human identity is marked by repressed sexuality, deeply imbedded into us from childhood experiences, which leads to psychological unease and unrest. Religion and religious experiences, argues Freud, are ways in which we attempt to deal with our psychological needs, but are simply childlike desires for a good relationship with a father figure (God), and they actually avoid us coming to terms, and dealing properly with our needs. **MARX** suggested that religion acts like an opiate to dull the

pain people feel in daily life caused by lack of economic power. **JAMES** argued that such a dismissal of religious experiences arose from those who were already deeply hostile to religion. Furthermore, many who have been committed to the cause of their religion, strengthened by their religious experiences, have found religion to be far from an opiate but something that has led to them being persecuted and even martyred.

4. **FLEW** - Suggests that it is not possible to give any credence to statements such as "I saw the risen Christ", due to the fact that there is no test by which we can assess if such a statement is true or not; verification and falsification are both impossible and therefore the statement is meaningless.

5. **KANT** - Argued that it is simply not possible to experience things beyond the phenomenal realm as we do not have any senses that can access a noumenal realm. Such may exist, but "given that human senses are finite and limited, it is impossible for humans to experience an unlimited God". (**EYRE** et al)

KEY QUOTES

1. *"Religious experience seems to the subject to be an experience of God or of some other supernatural being." Richard Swinburne*

2. *"In the natural sciences and industrial arts, it never occurs to anyone to try to refute opinions by showing up their author's neurotic constitution." William James*

3. *"From a scientific point of view, we can make no distinction between the man who eats little and sees heaven and the man who drinks much and sees snakes." Bertrand Russell*

4. *"To say that God spoke to him in a dream, is no more than to say that he dreamed God spoke to him." Hobbes*

5. *"Religion is the feelings, acts, and experiences of individual men in their solitude in relation to whatever they many consider the divine." William James*

6. *"God establishes himself in the interior of this soul in such a way it is wholly impossible for me to doubt that I have been in God, and God in me." Teresa of Ávila*

7. *"The fact that a belief has a good moral effect upon a man is no evidence whatsoever in its favour." Bertrand Russell*

8. *"How things seem to be is good grounds for a belief about how things are." Richard Swinburne*

CONFUSIONS TO AVOID

1. **WRONG CONCLUSION** - James did not state that religious experiences proved the existence of God. He did state that the experience was "real" (you can discuss what "real" means), and he did say more than the fact that religious experiences are passive, ineffable, noetic and transient. I have read many essays that outline **P.I.N.T.** as this was all that James said about religious experiences. His conclusions are far more wide-ranging.

2. **PSYCHOLOGICAL QUESTIONS** - This particular topic has many links with psychology, and things such as how accurate our memory of events are (see brilliant treatment of this in The Invisible Gorilla and other ways our intuitions deceive us), how we can access other minds and what it means to have a psychological experience. The challenge for the philosophy student is to see if religious experience stands up to **PHILOSOPHICAL** scrutiny. The examiner will not expect, or want you to produce a psychological critique of religious experiences.

3. **FALLACY** - Students can be prone to commit the "fallacy of the excluded middle" in this topic: a religious experience is either real or an illusion (ie false). There might be another sort of **MIDDLE** experience going on, so that it is not entirely illusory that "something" happened. How one argues this **EXCLUDED MIDDLE** presents difficulties, but that goes right to the core of this particular subject.

4. **TRUTH CONDITIONS** - A reasonable way in which to assess visions and voices and other types of religious experience, is to see if they:

    a. fit in with the general teaching of the religion and

    b. lead to an outcome that accords with the teaching of that religion.

    This widens out the analysis from that specific experience; however, whether it says anything about the "truth" of that particular experience might depend on what one thinks of the "truth" of the religion.

5. **EYRE ET AL** - They rightly point out that there is a difference in saying: "If there is a God there are likely to be experiences of him" (a claim **SWINBURNE** makes) and "there are religious experiences, therefore there is a God". The former statement is less controversial though not necessarily true. The latter commits the fallacy of affirming the consequent (the consequent is the second half of the statement, or the consequence if the first half of the statement is the case). It is like saying, "I have a wet house, therefore it is raining", whereas there could be many other reasons why I have a wet house, such as my neighbour watering his prize roses. There might be religious experiences, but one cannot conclude from these that there is a God.

REVELATION AND HOLY SCRIPTURE

Revelation can come in many ways - through nature and conscience - known as **GENERAL REVELATION**, and through personal encounter with the "wholly other", religious experience(s) and through **HOLY SCRIPTURE** - the latter examples being known as **SPECIAL REVELATION**.

Holy Scripture has authority within religious communities precisely because it is holy or "set apart", and is therefore "special revelation". There are groups within religions who take the actual commands of Holy Scripture in a literal sense, while others regard the Church or religious authorities as the bodies that can interpret the meaning of the text for today's world. Whilst accepting scripture as authoritative and of divine origin, the latter group argue that there is a need to interpret the commands and teachings in a way which maintains the intention of those laws and concurrently speaks relevantly to today's culture.

There are different ways of regarding revelation through scripture, two of which are **PROPOSITIONAL AND NON-PROPOSITIONAL REVELATION**. Scripture has authority in both these approaches, but in different ways. In fact, believers can sometimes hold that God reveals himself in both of these ways - propositionally through scripture, and non-propositionally through other and varied religious experiences and through nature itself.

PROPOSITIONAL REVELATION refers to how God reveals his nature to people through propositions or truths in His Word. God's Word is inerrant (without error) because it has been verbally inspired by God. These truths or propositions are statements of fact that reveal things about God. The Qur'an is regarded as propositional revelation, whilst elements within Christianity regard biblical revelation as taking the form of propositions. The believer accepts these revelations because they are from God and such truths are not accepted due to their logic or because humans can use **REASON** to work them out. This means that for some who accept propositional revelation, the biblical or Qur'anic stories are exactly like they say they are (ie the creation stories), even if scientific evidence suggests otherwise.

However, **TAYLOR** notes that, for many believers, the use of reason is not rejected, but that, for those that believe in propositional revelation, "God's revelations are not provable by reason". Indeed, the Roman Catholic position, whilst propositional, stresses the idea that God has revealed his laws through reason and this will align with the Word of God, which still needs to be interpreted to speak to Christians today. It is important to note that one can take a propositional approach to Scripture without interpreting the Bible literally in a word for word manner. **AQUINAS** argued that God can also be revealed in the world through **NATURAL THEOLOGY**, such as evidence of causation in the world that leads to the idea of a first cause. Again, these natural revelations will agree with the propositional revelation God makes of himself in scripture.

A person who accepts propositional revelation will regard scripture as the **WORD OF GOD** in which the authors are passive recipients of God's revelation to humanity. The authors were under the direction of God to record his revelation, and these revelations reveal God's nature and will. The Bible is regarded as "divinely spoken"/the Word of God. However, some who regard scripture as propositional revelation also believe that the authors have a role in recording the revelation in their own language and styles. Indeed, there are passages where the human voice is very strongly in evidence (see Psalm 51); many Christians view this as divinely inspired, but would not take out the human element from it. This is in contrast to a more fundamentalist position in which the authors are passive channels through which God delivers his word. Both these views regard scripture as without error in revealing God's will and nature.

NON-PROPOSITIONAL KNOWLEDGE is not factual in nature, but refers to a different sort or sorts of knowledge such as the skill to do something like driving a car or speaking in another language. Non-propositional revelation refers to the knowledge of God which is seen through what he has done in the world, or through his guidance, or through the example of Christ. Taylor notes, that, in this view, the believer recognises the actions of God in history and human experience. This evidence which leads to the belief that God has acted is both **INTERPRETATIVE** and **INDIRECT**.

With regard to Holy Scripture, non-propositional revelation refers to the way in which God is seen to have acted in history, as recorded by people through their experiences. Non-propositional revelation revolves around **FAITH IN** something rather than **FAITH THAT** something is the case. **BUBER** stressed the need to view faith as an I-Thou relationship, rather than in an I-It sense, where truth-seeking propositional-type questions about "what God is" are replaced by "who art Thou?", and the stress is on a relational rather than a factual approach.

Those who wrote about Christ or witnessed his work interpreted such events, through faith, as God's work, as does the believer when they read the record of it. If the Bible is regarded as non-propositional revelation, the role of the reader and how the reader interprets the Bible will be of crucial importance, because the non-propositional revelation takes place in the life of the believer. You should note here the differences between this and the propositional/Truth way of regarding Scripture, where the role of the author and reader of holy text is limited to a more passive reception of the revelation of the Word of God.

To stress, the author and the reader play a vital role in the non-propositional approach to revelation and faith becomes a way of seeing and interpreting the world. Christ is received by faith from the "inspired words of the Bible", rather than through acceptance of propositional truth statements from the Word of God, as the reader interprets the text and story.

The Bible is seen to point to Christ, the Word of God, rather than be the Word of God itself.

SCHLEIERMACHER was associated with this approach, which stressed the need for the experiential in the religious life. **TAYLOR** notes that in Schleiermacher's approach Christ was regarded as someone who raised awareness of God rather than one to be accepted propositionally as the one who saves people.

BARTH strongly rejected this view, arguing that God alone, not nature or reason, provides knowledge through revelation. When attempts are made to combine faith and reason to understand the revelation of God, as seen in the work of **AQUINAS**, Barth argued that people quickly go wrong. Barth's claim that divine revelation is not the same as human insight, notes **AHLUWALIA**, limits God's revelation to his action, not human interpretation.

STRENGTHS

1. **UNCHANGING** - If God is unchanging and has revealed his will and nature, then propositional revelation gives an account of a set of teachings and laws which do not change according to the latest human fads. God is given due regard as one who is the eternal source of right revelation, not interpreted by fallible humanity; this also means right moral decisions can be made according to the guidance of propositional revelation.

2. **TRUE TO GOD** - The propositional account gives a high status to the Word of God as infallible, ie, without error, which one might expect if it is revelation from God.

3. **FLEXIBLE** - Non-propositional revelation gives due regard to the idea that the reader of the Bible can use their capacity to interpret and understand it in a way which retains their freedom. The reader is seen to be active in the receipt and interpretation of revelation which respects their dignity and enables them to see the Bible as part of life, deeply influential upon their worldview and adopted through their freely chosen faith response to it.

WEAKNESSES

1. **IMPLAUSIBLE** - Can we ever be truly passive in our psyche when receiving revelation? Is there always an interpretive element to it? Can we be sure that the revelation humanity is purported to have received through God's propositional disclosure is as God intended, and how do we know if the authors have remembered such revelation correctly when memory can play tricks?

2. **REJECTED** - Can we ever be sure what a true proposition is and what is not? What about the different truth claims that are made both within, and between, religions, for example, about the status of Jesus Christ as either the Son of God in Christianity or a prophet in Islam? How can propositional revelation stay relevant when some of the views revealed in scripture have been seen to be rejected by many modern-day societies?

3. **READER RELATIVE** - Non-propositional revelation puts too much emphasis on the interpretation of the event by the reader. There are no infallible "facts" over which one is in dispute; the reader interprets what the biblical text reveals, and in what way he interprets the world as a non-propositional revelation of God. There are many different ways of looking at the world if no facts are revealed and it is difficult to know why one worldview should be seen as more authoritative than another, which is very different to those who regard revelation as propositional. However, **WILKINSON** and **CAMPBELL** point out that there is a link between the two types of revelation because people don't just believe, non-propositionally, in something (Latin "fiducia") without paying regard to what ("fides") that something is propositionally - many people believe that the Word of God is to be accepted propositionally whilst "believing no less fervently in Jesus as personal Saviour".

KEY QUOTES

1. *"Revealed theology concerns those truths about God which are only knowable through God's special revelation, such as the Trinity or the divine nature of Jesus. This distinction is generally rejected by those who hold a non-propositional view."* Wilkinson and Campbell.

2. *"Since the creation of the world, his invisible qualities, his eternal power and divine nature, have been clearly seen, being understood through what he has made."* Paul on General Revelation. *"All Scripture is God-breathed and is useful for teaching, rebuking, correcting and training in righteousness."* 1 Timothy 3:16, on Special Revelation

3. Muslims believe that *"when a person who is not necessarily a believer reads the Qur'an sincerely and without ulterior motives, they readily recognise that it is a holy book and are converted. The propositions in the Qur'an have such power because they are dictated by Gabriel to the Prophet."* The Bible never makes this claim - it was written by many authors from stories spanning centuries

4. *"The distinction between propositional and non-propositional approaches is theologically and philosophically valuable, but it is not the whole story of faith as lived."* Wilkinson and Campbell

CONFUSIONS TO AVOID

1. The propositionalist position is not a literalist position. The Roman Catholic approach accepts that the Bible is the Word of God whilst recognising the need to understand the time, culture and intentions of the authors.

2. Propositional revelation can be viewed as "belief that such a proposition is true, whereas non-proposition makes reference to belief in someone, as a statement of trust, involving a commitment rather than intellectual assent." (**WILKINSON** and **CAMPBELL**) Non-propositional revelation can be "conveyed ... through art, music, dance, metaphor and symbol". (**AHLUWALIA**)

3. Don't say of the Bible that because something is not "true" in a literal sense it can be dismissed as having no meaning, as different genres in the Bible, such as poetry and prophecy, are interpreted differently.

Psychology and Religion

KEY TERMS

- **ARCHETYPE** - In Jungian psychology, the part of the mind responsible for creating images.

- **COLLECTIVE NEUROSIS** - A neurotic illness that affects all people.

- **COLLECTIVE UNCONSCIOUS** - In Jung's understanding of the division of the mind, the collective unconscious is the component of the mind which is common to all humans.

- **CONSCIOUS MIND** - The component of the mind which contains everything within our present awareness.

- **ILLUSION** - An idea, image or belief created by the mind in order to satisfy a particular longing or desire. The term "illusion" is not intended to highlight that the idea, image or belief is false, but that it stems from human wishes.

- **INDIVIDUATION** - In Jungian psychology, the process of becoming an individual through the balancing of the different components of the mind.

- **NEUROSIS** - A type of psychological disorder. The term represents a range of mental disorders in which an emotional distress or unconscious conflict manifests itself in anxiety and is visible through some form of physical behaviour.

- **PERSONAL UNCONSCIOUS** - In Jung's understanding of the division of the mind, the personal unconscious is the component of the mind which contains past memories.

- **PSYCHE** - The term to define all the components, both conscious and unconscious, of the mind.

- **PSYCHIC ENERGY** - The energy by which the work of the mind is done.

- **REPRESSION** - In Freudian psychology, the process of burying unwanted or unpleasant thoughts within the unconscious mind.

- **SUBLIMATION** - In Freudian psychology, the process by which the energy behind sexual impulses is transferred into other, more socially acceptable, activities.

- **UNCONSCIOUS MIND** - The component of the mind which contains our base drives and automatic processes.

- **WISH FULFILMENT** - The process of creating an illusion to satisfy a particular longing which stems from human wishes.

FREUD'S THEORY OF RELIGION

Religion as a neurosis

Sigmund Freud (1856-1939) believed that religion is an **ILLUSION** created by the mind in order to satisfy particular longings and overcome psychological conflict as well as the fear and helplessness naturally felt by humans.

Freud worked with patients suffering from **NEUROSES**. These patients presented themselves to him with a range of physical symptoms, including obsessive behaviour, pain, hysteria and phobia. His work with these patients was critical in forming his understanding of the mind being comprised of both **CONSCIOUS** and **UNCONSCIOUS** parts. At the same time, his work using hypnosis led him to the conclusion that the **UNCONSCIOUS MIND** contains the memories of long-forgotten events. For Freud, it was the unpleasant memories held within the **UNCONSCIOUS MIND** which were presenting themselves in the form of the physical behaviour of his patients.

Freud believed that the neurotic behaviours presented by his patients were similar to the behaviours easily observed in religious people. Often, his patients would perform highly obsessive actions such as compulsive hand washing and this, for example, could be compared with religious washing rituals.

Upon entering the church, before the start of a service, members from a range of Christian denominations will make the sign of the cross after having first dipped their hand in holy water. A particular sequence of movements must be followed each time, moving the right hand from the forehead to the stomach and then to touch the left and right shoulders in turn. The movements can also be accompanied by reciting specific words, usually "In the name of the Father, and of the Son, and of the Holy Spirit, Amen". Whilst there might be different interpretations of the meaning of this act, it is clear that there is a great significance to it.

Similarly, other religious acts have great significance. In the Roman Catholic Church, the Sacrament of Penance, which is more commonly known as Confession, should be received at least once a year. The act of Confession is likely to appear meaningless to a non-member of the Church but for a Roman Catholic it is an essential ritual as it allows them to cleanse their soul so that they might go to heaven after they die. Not attending Confession regularly could cause a Roman Catholic to experience feelings of severe guilt and to regard the Sacrament with ambivalence.

Freud concluded that, just as his patients' behavioural symptoms were a result of trauma buried within the **UNCONSCIOUS MIND**, religious behaviour was also a symptom revealing some buried trauma; trauma which was presenting itself in the form of a **NEUROSIS** - religion itself.

Neurosis as a result of trauma which is sexual in nature

Freud believed that the trauma from which a **NEUROSIS** stemmed was always sexual in nature. His study of the **PSYCHE** led him to think that sexual drive had the highest capability of causing disruption to psychological development as the subconscious urge to achieve satisfaction would inevitably lead to problems. According to Freud, each individual suffers from the **OEDIPUS COMPLEX**. He describes the feelings of jealousy and hatred which a child comes to feel as the attention they receive from their mother, which as a suckling infant seems sole and complete, is recognised, as they grow older, as being shared with their father. Their father becomes their rival and the child becomes overwhelmed with the desire to kill them so that they alone may possess their mother. This desire, combined with the respect and fear they have felt for their father previously, causes feelings of **AMBIVALENCE**. It is this which is the **OEDIPUS COMPLEX**.

The child is unable to carry out the desire to kill their father and this conflict becomes buried deep in the **UNCONSCIOUS MIND**. This **REPRESSION** is not fully effective and, as the mind continues to attempt to resolve the conflict, it is not possible to prevent memories resurfacing in the **CONSCIOUS MIND**. This resurfacing happens in the form of neurotic behaviour, with one such behaviour being religion.

Freud attempted to support his theory by using the work of Charles Darwin to show that the **OEDIPUS COMPLEX** had historically affected society; this would be Freud's justification of religion as a **COLLECTIVE NEUROSIS**, because guilt could be passed genetically to one's descendants.

Freud suggested that primitive societies were arranged in **HORDES**; groups centred around a dominant male figure. Within these hordes, the younger males would become jealous of the power of the dominant male until they grouped together with the intention to kill him. Whilst having hatred of his power, the group would also remember the respect they had for the dominant male when they were younger and this would result in feelings of ambivalence. Freud argued that the strength of these feelings would cause the younger males to idolise the dominant male and make him the **TOTEM** of their group.

Religion resulting from buried trauma

Freud proposed a two-stage development of repressed trauma into religion. The first stage, **ANIMISM**, came about when those feeling the guilt from their trauma began to invest objects such as animals, rocks or trees with spirits, thereby creating a **TOTEM** object toward which the guilt could be transferred and amends could attempt to be made.

The **TOTEM** became the symbolic father figure and therefore would be regarded with the same ambivalence felt towards the father. The mixture of hatred and reverence would be played out in rituals surrounding the **TOTEM ANIMAL**, with a particular focus on those which involved symbolic killing and eating of the totem animal.

The second stage is the development into religion and this largely happens because of the dissatisfaction felt with the **TOTEM OBJECT**. As time passed, the reputation of the father became so embellished that he became a god-like figure to the group. Freud believed that it can be seen in religion that God is regarded with the same ambivalence as was the father and the totem object and that this proves a link. He drew attention to the example of the Christian God who, whilst regarded with deference for the most part, would be regularly killed and eaten as part of the Communion Rite.

Religion as wish fulfilment and reaction against helplessness

Through his explanation of the **OEDIPUS COMPLEX**, Freud believed that he had demonstrated his original premise that religion was wish fulfilment.

He went on to argue that the nature of society made it necessary to construct the **ILLUSION** of religion. If individuals acted upon their basic longings then society would not be able to operate because there would be a lack of control and order. In addition, religion gives individuals a reason to control their behaviour because they have to answer to an omnipotent, omniscient God who would make judgements on their actions. As well as the threat of punishment, there is also the promise of reward for good behaviour and this makes it bearable for the individual to control their basic longings.

The process of **SUBLIMATION** is one in which the energy behind sexual impulses, the basic longings of individuals, is transferred into more socially acceptable activities. Religion motivates this process because it provides outlets for the energy and rewards involvement in activities such as charity work or producing religious art or music.

In addition, religion serves the purpose of helping individuals to overcome their fears of the natural world. Humans inevitably feel small and defenceless when confronted by natural forces, including death. The existence of an omnipotent, omniscient God is comforting because it gives a sense of protection against what cannot be controlled. In this case, religion is **WISH FULFILMENT** because it satisfies the longing to be looked after.

WEAKNESSES OF FREUD'S THEORY

There are very few scholars who would accept Freud's theory of religion. The following weaknesses have been identified:

- Freud lacks **EVIDENCE** for his theory. Many of his conclusions are formed from speculation and he could not provide any anthropological evidence for his assertions about primitive societies and ambivalence towards **TOTEM** objects. There is also no evidence to suggest that guilt can be transferred to descendants.

- Freud presented a mere five case studies in support of his theory, and this narrow selection of evidence can be criticised. His theory aimed to be an explanation of all forms of religion but, in actual fact, he failed to take account of religions other than the male dominant Jewish and Christian traditions with which he was familiar.

- The **OEDIPUS COMPLEX** has been discredited as a universal neurosis, and Bronislaw Malinowski has suggested that such a complex might actually be caused as a result of strict religious rules, rather than be the initial cause of those rules.

- Freud's theory does not acknowledge that there could be any benefit to believing in religion. He sees it as an entirely negative **ILLUSION** and this idea has been criticised by scholars who point out that, almost regardless of its factual truth, religion can be of benefit to those who believe in it and those positives ought to be credited.

JUNG'S THEORY OF RELIGION

Rejection of Freud

Carl Gustav Jung (1875-1961) presents a psychological explanation of religion which is opposed to that of Freud. He did accept that religion was a creation of the **PSYCHE** but argued that it was essential in producing a balanced mind.

Jung rejected Freud's conclusion that neuroses were caused by repressed sexual trauma and, instead, argued that, in cases where the whole of an individual's personality was affected, it was the disturbance of **PSYCHIC ENERGY** which was the cause of a neurosis.

Jung's concept of the mind

From his work with patients, Jung noted that there were similarities between the images with which dreamers, or sufferers of psychic disorders, would see and describe. This observation led Jung to suggest that the **UNCONSCIOUS MIND** had two components: the **PERSONAL UNCONSCIOUS** and the **COLLECTIVE UNCONSCIOUS**. The first of these contained an individual's past memories and the second was shared by all humans; shared, not in the sense that we inherit this part of our unconscious from our ancestors, but in the sense that all humans have this same part of their **UNCONSCIOUS MIND** which, in each of them, performs the same function.

He argued that the **COLLECTIVE UNCONSCIOUS** performs the function of creating images, the type of which may appear in dreams or which may affect those suffering from a psychic disorder. The

COLLECTIVE UNCONSCIOUS includes a series of **ARCHETYPES** which are responsible for generating types of images and, due to the nature of the **COLLECTIVE UNCONSCIOUS** being shared by all humans, it is therefore inevitable that there will be similarities in the images experienced by individuals.

The archetypes and individuation

The **PERSONA ARCHETYPE** is linked to the representation of one's self to the world, and Jung understood this as the mask that an individual wears in order to make one's personality more appropriate for society.

The **SHADOW ARCHETYPE** is linked to the darker side of personality, where negative characteristics which an individual might deny to themselves become confused and cause chaos for the personality.

The **ANIMUS** and **ANIMA ARCHETYPES** are linked to the opposite sex, where the first presents the masculine side of the female personality and the second presents the female side of the masculine personality.

The **GOD ARCHETYPE** is essential to understanding Jung's theory of religion, as he argued that each individual has an inbuilt function of their **PSYCHE** to create religious images. These images are, initially, of a general appearance but then become shaped by the personal experiences of the individual. For example, the **GOD ARCHETYPE** produces a general image of an omnipotent and omniscient figure but, for someone born in the Western World into a Christian family, this appears in a dream or psychic disorder as the God figure typical of the Western Christian tradition.

For Jung, God is a very real expression of the **COLLECTIVE UNCONSCIOUS** and this led him to argue that there can be truth to an individual's experience of God. Jung stated that he could not explain the ultimate cause of the **GOD ARCHETYPE** and therefore could not assert anything positive or negative about the existence of God, but he believed that there could be genuine religious experience because, to the individual, the image generated of God could be so powerful as to cause them to change, or re-evaluate, their life. Jung in fact argued that any experience of any of the **ARCHETYPES** was a religious experience because these experiences met the criteria of being deeply personal to the individual, ineffable in nature and all equally capable of causing a change in lifestyle.

The **SELF ARCHETYPE** is the tendency of each individual to want to become whole, and this **ARCHETYPE** governs the process of **INDIVIDUATION** which, for Jung, was the process of balancing the components of the mind and becoming whole - becoming an individual. The individuation process is important because the work of the mind is done by **PSYCHIC ENERGY** and, if the process is not completed properly, it can result in a disrupted **PSYCHIC ENERGY** and, ultimately, an unbalanced and unhealthy mind.

Jung argued that **INDIVIDUATION** was a religious process because it was governed by the **ARCHETYPES** and any experience of the archetypes met the criteria of a religious experience. He also thought that religious images contributed towards the sense of wholeness that the process of individuation aimed to achieve. Rejecting religion would be to reject a substantial part of the process of individuation which would lead to an unbalanced mind and the possibility of experiencing a neurosis.

Jung's idea of **INDIVIDUATION** is not unfamiliar to religion, particularly religions from an Indian tradition. A study of Buddhist meditation shows similarities between the aims of this practice and the individuation process explained by Jung. The first four archetypes highlight the misconceptions held by an individual about their own personality and, through the process of individuation, Jung explains that the individual must come to terms with these misconceptions. Similarly, in Buddhist meditation, ignorance must be removed before progress can be made with the practice. The God **ARCHETYPE** generates images which help the process of individuation, moving towards wholeness, and, again, in Buddhist meditation there is often the need for an individual to have a positive image on which they can focus their meditative contemplation. The goal and benefit of individuation is clear; to achieve a balanced and healthy mind which would not be prone to neuroses. In Buddhism, the goal is also to achieve a sense of balance and the benefits of meditation to an individual's mental and physical health have long been recognised.

WEAKNESSES OF JUNG'S THEORY

Similarly to Freud's theory of religion, there have been serious criticisms of Jung. The following weaknesses have been identified:

- It has been suggested that Jung's view that it is impossible to know anything about God's existence is incorrect. He makes the assumption that it is impossible to know of anything beyond the psychic world and this **METHODOLOGY** has been questioned. Religious experiences should be subject to the same standards of verification as all other experiences.

- **GEZA ROHEIM** criticises the idea that the **ARCHETYPES** are responsible for similarities in religious imagery and points out that, given the many experiences shared by all humans, it is inevitable that there are similarities between the myths and stories from a range of cultures and religions. Equally the explanation of the God **ARCHETYPE** does not take into account the fact that many people have no religious belief whatsoever and Jung, when presented with this criticism, has no satisfactory response.

- Jung argues for a type of **RELIGIOUS EXPERIENCE** which many people disagree with. Martin Buber states that an experience of the mind is not a religious experience and that there is no justification for the classification of any **ARCHETYPAL** image as a religious experience.

- Similarly the explanation of **INDIVIDUATION** as a religious process can be questioned. Jung links the process to the **SELF ARCHETYPE** which has no direct link to God or religion. To suggest that religious images give help to the balancing of one's mind is to understate the role and significance of religion for a believer.

KEY ISSUES

- Has God been "explained away" by psychology?

- What are the strengths and weaknesses of psychological views of religion?

- What is the relationship between religion and mental health?

KEY QUOTES

1. *"At the bottom of every case of hysteria there are one or more occurrences of premature sexual experience." Freud, The Aetiology of Hysteria*

2. *"Religion would thus be the universal obsessional neurosis of humanity." Freud, The Future of an Illusion*

3. *Religious teachings are ... "Fulfillments of the oldest, strongest and most urgent wishes of mankind. The secret of their strength lies in the strength of those wishes." Freud, The Future of an Illusion*

4. *"Freud found no reason to believe in God and therefore saw no value or purpose in the rituals of religious life ... Freud is certain that religious beliefs are erroneous; they are superstitions." Daniel L Pals, Seven Theories of Religion*

5. *"Almost all the evidence that Freud presents has been discredited in one way or another." Michael Palmer, Freud and Jung*

6. *"It seems that the verdict must be 'not proven' ... The Freudian theory of religion may be true but has not been shown to be so." Hick, Philosophy of Religion*

7. *"We simply do not know the ultimate derivation of the archetype any more than we know the origin of the psyche ... Nothing positive or negative has thus been asserted about the possible existence of any God." Jung, Psychology and Alchemy*

8. *"The symbols of divinity coincide with those of the self: what, on the one side, appears as a psychological experience, signifying psychic wholeness, expresses on the other side the idea of God."* Jung, *Civilisation in Transition*

9. Jung *"May have uncovered one of the mechanisms by which God creates an idea of the deity in the human mind."* Hick, *Philosophy of Religion*

10. *"A large proportion of thinkers take a well reasoned middle ground, maintaining that religion has the potential to be either positive or negative in its effects on mental ill health."* Schumaker, *Religion and Mental Health*

Atheism and Postmodernism

KEY TERMS

- **AGNOSTICISM** - The belief that there is not sufficient knowledge to be able to prove or deny that God exists.

- **ATHEISM** - The belief that there is no God.

- **CULTURAL CONSTRUCTS** - The idea that beliefs, religious or otherwise, are a product of the cultures from which they stem.

- **META-NARRATIVE** - A "grand story" which claims to have an absolute and truthful explanation of reality.

- **MORAL ABSOLUTISM** - The ethical view that some actions are always right or always wrong, regardless of the particular situation or circumstances.

- **NEGATIVE ATHEISM/WEAK ATHEISM** - The personal belief that there is no God, without a denial that God exists.

- **POSITIVE ATHEISM/STRONG ATHEISM** - The personal belief that there is no God, with a denial that God exists.

- **POSTMODERNISM** - The view that there can be truth in a range of different explanations of reality; there is not one meta-narrative.

- **RELIGIOUS PLURALISM** - The view that there is not one, true, religion but that there are many religions which hold some truth and value.

- **SITUATION ETHICS** - A consequentialist ethical theory which states that, in any situation, the morally correct action is that which best shows love.

- **VERIFICATION PRINCIPLE** - The principle which states that the only way to know the meaningfulness of a statement is to know how it may be proved true or false.

ATHEISM AND AGNOSTICISM

The word **ATHEISM** stems from two Greek words and means "without God". The popular definition of the word is taken to be the position that there is no God, but this does not take into account the actual range of positions an **ATHEIST** could take.

A **NEGATIVE ATHEIST**, also known as a **WEAK ATHEIST**, would deny having a personal belief in God but would not go so far as to deny, outright, the existence of God.

A **POSITIVE ATHEIST**, also known as a **STRONG ATHEIST**, would deny having a personal belief in God and deny, outright, the existence of god.

The word **AGNOSTICISM** stems from the Greek words meaning "without knowledge". An **AGNOSTIC** would have a viewpoint very similar to that of a **NEGATIVE ATHEIST**, denying having a personal belief in God but not denying, outright, the existence of God on the grounds that it is not possible to know enough in order to prove or deny the existence of God. Within this there might be some division of opinion, and Michael Martin names these two sub-beliefs **SCEPTICAL AGNOSTICISM** and **CANCELLATION AGNOSTICISM**.

A **SCEPTICAL AGNOSTIC** would argue that there is equally no good basis for believing that God exists or for denying that God exists. A **CANCELLATION AGNOSTIC** would argue that there is an equally good basis for believing that God exists and for denying that God exists. In both cases, the resulting position for the individual is that there is not enough information in order to prove or deny that God exists. In this way, **AGNOSTICISM** is opposed to the belief of **POSITIVE ATHEISM**.

REASONS FOR THE RISE OF ATHEISM AND RELIGIOUS RESPONSES

Science

Developments in modern science have been cited as a major contributing factor in the rise of atheism. Much of what was unknown about the world, for example its position within the universe, its origins and the development of human life, had been attributed to God and explained through religious stories. In this way, God can be seen as a **"GOD OF THE GAPS"**, filling in as an answer in areas where scientific knowledge was lacking.

Alistair McGrath explains three reasons why science has been a contributor to the rise of **ATHEISM**:

1. Science and religion are commonly presented as being in opposition to one another, with one founded on rational principles and the other on authoritarian beliefs.

2. Science provides evidence for its assertions and this has led many to ask religions to provide similar evidence for theirs.

3. Darwin's theory of evolution provides an explanation for the origins of human life which contradicts the widely held religious view of human life as the pinnacle of God's creative process.

As scientific developments have led to the answering of questions about the world, God has been pushed out of the gaps he filled. His role as an answer to questions about the world has gradually been diminished and religion has been brought into question because it cannot provide convincingly objective evidence for its beliefs. This trend for replacing religious belief with scientific fact has given rise to the opinion that, eventually, all questions will be answered by science; there will be no place for God in the generally accepted understanding of the world and, therefore, no reason to believe in Him.

Religious responses to science

It can be claimed that there is no scientific development which definitively proves that God does not exist. Many religions claim that their beliefs are, in fact, compatible with science because the two are answering different types of question. Science explains "how" things happen, or are the way they are. Religion explains "why" things happen, or are the way they are. Taking this view, it is perfectly possible to be, for example, a devout Christian and believe the Genesis creation stories whilst at the same time accepting that evolution explains how human life was formed.

Empiricism

EMPIRICISM goes hand in hand with science as a reason for the rise of atheism. It is the view that it is only possible to know that which can be experienced through the five senses and, therefore, can be **EMPIRICALLY VERIFIED**.

Empirical knowledge is the basis for scientific developments and it leads to an obvious criticism of belief in God because God cannot be experienced through the five senses and therefore cannot be **EMPIRICALLY VERIFIED**.

This view can be linked with the philosophical movement of the **LOGICAL POSITIVISTS** and AJ Ayer's **VERIFICATION PRINCIPLE**, which claims that the only way to know the meaningfulness of a statement is to know how it may be proved true or false. Using this principle, as it is not possible to know what would prove the existence or non-existence of God it is therefore meaningless to discuss the possible existence or non-existence of God.

Religious responses to empiricism

Religions can counter **EMPIRICISM** in three ways. Firstly, by highlighting that many religious experiences are **EMPIRICAL** in nature and therefore can be tested as proof for God's existence. Secondly, by questioning the view of **EMPIRICISM** that it is only possible to have knowledge through the five senses. Experiences of our emotions, for example love, are non-empirical but it would not be suggested that these emotions are unknowable and therefore not real. Religions can point to this and argue that experience of God is similar in that it is both knowable and real but not open to empirical verification. Finally, religions can look to the generally accepted definition of God. If God were to be real he would be all that is non-empirical and this would explain why it is not possible to test or verify His existence; He is, by nature, beyond the scope of such testing. Although this argument is likely to be dissatisfactory to many, it is also a fairly logical criticism. It is not fair to deny that God exists because He does not meet the testing we would like to impose upon Him, when it is logically impossible for a God with the characteristics generally ascribed to Him to be tested in such a way.

The **VERIFICATION PRINCIPLE** is also open to criticism because, as a statement, it itself does not meet the necessary criteria to be considered meaningful.

The problem of evil

The **PROBLEM OF EVIL** is one of the most convincing reasons for an individual to adopt atheism. The problem states that it is logically impossible for an **OMNIPOTENT**, **OMNIBENEVOLENT** God to exist in a world where evil exists. As we know that evil, both **MORAL** and **NATURAL**, exists in our world then it must be the case that an **OMNIPOTENT**, **OMNIBENEVOLENT** God does not also exist.

It is impossible to deny the existence of evil in the world. Particularly so in the modern age where **MEDIA** allows individuals to know about the suffering which takes place across the world, as well as in their own lives.

Attempts to reconcile the existence of God with the existence of evil can be dissatisfactory as they suggest that there is a good reason for evil, though humans could not know what this is, that evil is a punishment for sin or that evil might be necessary in order to achieve a greater good. It can be said that these attempts fail to overcome the question of why, knowing the evil that would happen, God would create the world in the way that He did. God, it seems, was either incapable of creating a better world or did not want to create a better world and both of these conclusions are incompatible with traditional theistic belief in an omnipotent and omnibenevolent God.

Religious responses to the problem of evil

As already noted, there have been many attempts to reconcile the existence of an omnipotent and omnibenevolent God with the existence of evil in the world. The majority of these use **FREE WILL** as a justification for evil. God created humans with free will so that they could choose for themselves to do good actions and follow God, rather than be like robots programmed always to choose to do good actions and follow God. Religions argue that it is necessary that humans have **FREE WILL** but, by its very nature, this then allows for them to choose to do evil, rather than good, and turn away from God, rather than follow Him. It is this misuse of **FREE WILL** which is the cause of the evil in the world. Scholars have also suggested that evil is necessary in order for humans to choose to do good because, without evil, there would be no opportunity to show love or compassion to others.

The rebellion against moral absolutes

MORAL ABSOLUTISTS hold the view that there are some actions which are always right or always wrong, regardless of the particular situation or circumstances. In the 20th C and 21st C there has been a sharp decline in the number of people who hold to this view, and even some religions themselves have introduced a degree of **RELATIVITY** into their moral teachings.

A particularly good example of the decline in moral absolutes is that of unmarried couples cohabiting. In the post-war decades couples rebelled against traditional rules and chose to cohabit before, or instead of, being married. This trend has continued steadily into the present and, as a result, has become socially acceptable with phrases such as "living in sin" no longer being used to describe a cohabiting unmarried couple. The

Church of England is one example of a religious organisation which has shown support to those of its followers who choose to cohabit without being married.

Rebellion against **MORAL ABSOLUTES** has contributed to the rise of atheism, because rejecting moral absolutes has meant rejecting the authority from which the rules come. As HP Owen states, commands must have a commander and, therefore, if the validity of the command is discredited so the validity of the commander is also discredited.

Religious responses to the rebellion against moral absolutes

Some religions have embraced the idea that morality is more **RELATIVIST** than it is **ABSOLUTIST**. The Church of England is a particular example of how a religion has reinterpreted its moral teachings in light of modern standards of right and wrong. This approach has been influenced by **SITUATION ETHICS** which, as a Christian ethical theory, is based upon the teachings of Jesus and is compatible with belief in God but encourages consideration of each situation rather than prescribing fixed rules to be followed at all times. It can be said that the turning away from moral absolutes does not undermine religion because religion itself is going through the same process of reinterpreting right and wrong in the modern world. It is possible to go further than this and suggest that moral absolutes are not being abandoned but merely replaced by a more flexible set of rules. The moral absolute in situation ethics is to always "love thy neighbour", but the system recognises that this love may be different depending on circumstances.

Awareness of other faiths

Although awareness of **OTHER FAITHS** is not new, in the 20th C there has been more involvement and dialogue between faiths and this has lead to questioning of the **META-NARRATIVES** of each religion.

Each religion has its own stories and traditions which explain its beliefs and its view of the world. These stories and traditions are different between the religions and can be seen as contradictions of what each religion teaches to be the truth. For example, it cannot be the case that the creation story of each religion is true, for they are all different and therefore contradictory. This then leads to the question of which, or if indeed any, contain the truth.

DAVID HUME would argue that it is not difficult to move from the thought that all the religions cannot be true to the thought that none of them must be true. Each religion cancels out the claims of the others, meaning that there is more evidence against any particular claim of a religion being true than there is in favour of it being true. This leads to the inevitable conclusion that there is more reason to disbelieve the truth claims of a religion than there is to believe and that it would be more sensible to adopt an **ATHEIST** point of view.

Religious responses to the awareness of other faiths

Many religions have attempted to remove the conflict between themselves and other religions by adopting a **PLURALIST** point of view. This entails a religion recognising that there is not necessarily one true **META-NARRATIVE** to explain the world but that there are many versions of the truth contained within the different religions. Although each religion holds to its particular traditions, beliefs and practices, they acknowledge that there may be other routes to the same ultimate knowledge of God.

During the Second Vatican Council, the Roman Catholic Church produced "Nostra Aetate" - a declaration on the relationship of the Church with non-Christian religions. The document discusses Hinduism and Buddhism and states that the Roman Catholic Church "rejects nothing that is true and holy in these religions". It goes on to say that the Church regards the Islamic faith "with esteem" and that "it remembers the bond that spiritually ties the people of the New Covenant to Abraham's stock ... Indeed, the Church believes that by His cross Christ, our Peace, reconciled Jews and Gentiles, making both one in Himself."

THE MEANING OF THE SLOGAN "GOD IS DEAD"

In his 1882 work The Gay Science Friedrich Nietzsche wrote: "God is dead. God remains dead. And we have killed him." The meaning of this was not that God had physically lived and been killed but that society no longer had a use for God. It had developed in such a way as to make the position of God irrelevant to society.

Nietzsche's beliefs about God were tied to his beliefs about mankind and his belief that, for too long, humans had been fixated on projecting all that was good about their nature on to the figure of God. He felt that by unburdening humanity from God, humans would be able to focus on cultivating the "Ubermensch" - the "super human". This would allow for progress to be made in encouraging the development of humankind, rather than this being stalled by religion which preached that its followers shoukd accept their station in this life and, instead, look forward to a better afterlife.

POSTMODERNISM

POSTMODERNISM is a cultural viewpoint which can be understood as a reaction to the principle of modernity that there exists a single truth, a **META-NARRATIVE** which claims to have an absolute and truthful explanation of reality. **OS GUINNESS** suggests that **POSTMODERNISM** is a more modest point of view because it accepts that there can be truth in a variety of narratives. Holding a **POSTMODERNIST** viewpoint, there are four main ways in which religion can be viewed.

Religion as cultural constructs

Denying **META-NARRATIVES** means denying any claims to absolute truth - something which religions tend to do. The claims of religions therefore have to be understood in a different way, and it has been suggested that this understanding should be that religions are constructs of the cultures from which they stem. Emile Durkheim believed that religions represent the beliefs and attitudes of the societies they develop out of. The moral rules and behavioural expectations of a religion will be broadly in line with those acceptable within the society from which the religion develops and this explains why different religions, developing out of different societies, will have different rules and codes of conduct.

This view of religion also explains the differences within a religion which can be found in the followers of that religion who practise in different societies and cultures. For example, the variety of Islam practised in the Western world appears different to that practised in the Arab states, and this is further evidence of the relational link between culture and religion. Religion tends to reflect the norms and values of the culture in which it is practised and this can only be because society and religion are inter-linked.

No right or wrong religions

Following the rejection of any claims to absolute truth, it is only possible to conclude that there are no right and no wrong religions. For to claim that there are no right religions would be to adhere to the **META-NARRATIVE** of atheism which is as opposed to the principles of **POSTMODERNISM** as is claiming that there is one right religion. **POSTMODERNISM** is in line with the **PLURALIST** point of view because it accepts that there is truth and value in each and every religion. It is also **AGNOSTIC** in its point of view because of the acceptance that it just is not possible to know which, if any, claims about religion and God are true.

Religion as personal spiritual search

Accepting that there are no right and no wrong religions means that religion must be a more personal endeavour than a modernist viewpoint would hold. Religion is less about following a specific set of beliefs and practices taught by a religious organisation and more about pursuing one's own individual spiritual search. James Beckford writes about the modern-day "pick and mix" approach to religion where each individual chooses aspects of a religion which are appropriate to their lifestyle and to their aims for their religious belief. This type of spirituality, again, is in line with the **PLURALIST** idea that there might be many paths, all equally valid, to experiencing truth and, again, the **AGNOSTIC** view that it isn't possible to make a judgement on which claims about religion and God are true.

Living religion rather than intellectual faith

Given the **PLURALIST** and **AGNOSTIC** elements of the **POSTMODERN** view of religion, it is inevitable that, within this view of religion, emphasis is shifted from belief to action. It is not possible to know which, if any, belief claims about religion and God are true and therefore it is meaningless to base religion around these belief claims. It is better, instead, to focus on action and the living-out of beliefs in practical and productive ways which have a real-life visible benefit. From a **POSTMODERNIST** point of view, recitation of creeds is a misdirection of energy because it is impossible to know if those creeds contain any truth. To follow those creeds, for example by showing kindness, compassion and generosity to others, cannot be a misdirection of energy because the end product is a good one, regardless of whether or not the creed from which the motivation to act stemmed is true or false.

POSTMODERNISM AS AN AFFIRMATION OF RELIGION

- Many religions emphasise the importance of action over belief. Believers of all religions are encouraged to be witnesses to their faith.

- Many religions recognise the unknowable within their religions, and the **AGNOSTICISM** inherent within the postmodern point of view can be seen to reflect the emphasis within religions on having faith without proof.

- Some religious traditions are particularly well suited to the idea of not knowing. The mystical tradition of Christianity focused on gaining knowledge through intuition rather than through study or fact.

- Postmodernism exposes **ATHEISM** as a **META-NARRATIVE** which cannot be accepted and therefore weakens the case for rejecting, outright, belief in God.

POSTMODERNISM AS A THREAT TO RELIGION

- The belief that there can be no universal truth is a threat to those religions which present themselves as the one, true, religion.

- **AGNOSTICISM** can be a dissatisfactory point of view to take. Many, **THEISTS** and **ATHEISTS** alike, agree that there can be knowledge to prove or deny the existence of God.

- Taking the view that there can be many sources of truth can be dissatisfactory. It is more straightforward to argue that the different religions are opposed to each other and that their contradictions cancel out any claims to truth.

- The "pick and mix", consumerist, approach to religion is not encouraged by religious organisations as they, instead, encourage their followers to adhere to certain, specific, beliefs, practices and morals.

KEY ISSUES

- Is religion in retreat in the modern world?

- Is postmodernism an affirmation of religion?

- How successfully has religion responded to the challenge of atheism?

KEY QUOTES

1.   *"Science is 'The supreme catalyst' for the rise of atheism." Ray Billington, Religion without God*

2.   *"According to theological discourse, God is precisely that which is nonempirical." Gavin Hyman, The Cambridge Companion to Atheism*

3.   *"God is dead. God remains dead. And we have killed him." Nietzsche, The Gay Science*

4.   *"One of the last remaining bastions of atheism survives only at the popular level - namely, the myth that an atheistic, fact-based science is permanently at war with faith-based religion." McGrath, The Twilight of Atheism*

5.   *"Where modernism is a manifesto of human self-congratulation and self-confidence, postmodernism is a confession of modesty, if not despair." McGrath, The Twilight of Atheism*

6.   *"Theological meta-narratives are ruled out a priori by post-modernity." Wright, Postmodernism and Religion*

7.   *Postmodernism is "Not a particularly friendly environment for atheism ... If atheism is a metaphysical or an otherwise fixed and decisive denial of God." Caputo, The Cambridge Companion to Atheism*

8.　"At the modern supermarket of faith, the consumer seeks to pick and mix religious items to match their commitment and faith."
Beckford, Why Britain doesn't go to church

Exam Rescue Remedy

1. Build your own scaffolding which represents the logic of the theory. Use a mind map or a summary sheet.

2. Do an analysis of past questions by theme as well as by year. Try writing your own Philosophy of Religion paper based on what hasn't come up recently.

3. Examine examiners' reports (go to their website) for clues as to how to answer a question well.

4. List relevant technical vocabulary for inclusion in an essay (eg efficient cause, form of the good, analytic, synthetic).

5. Prepare key quotes from selected key authors, original/ contemporary - or even better, produce your own. Learn some.

6. Contrast and then evaluate different views/theories/authors, as some questions ask "which approach is best?" So contrast every approach with one other and decide beforehand what you think.

7. Practise writing for 35 minutes. Don't use a computer, unless you will do so in the exam.

8. Always answer and discuss the exact question in front of you; never learn a "model answer". Use your own examples (newspapers, films, documentaries, real life). Be prepared to think creatively and adapt your knowledge to the question.

9. Conclude with your view, and justify it (give reasons) - especially with "discuss".

Bibliography

- **AHLUWALIA, L** - Understanding Philosophy of Religion OCR, Folens, 2008

- **BOWIE, R** - AS/A2 Philosophy of Religion and Religious Ethics for OCR, Nelson Thornes, 2004

- **COLE, P** - Access to Philosophy: Philosophy of Religion, Hodder & Stoughton, 2005

- **DEWAR, G** - Oxford Revision Guides: AS & A Level Religious Studies: Philosophy and Ethics Through Diagrams, Oxford University Press, 2009

- **JACKSON, R** - The God of Philosophy, The Philosophers' Magazine, 2001

- **JORDAN, A, LOCKYER, N, TATE, E** - Philosophy of Religion for A Level OCR Edition, Nelson Thornes, 2004

- **PHELAN, JW** - Philosophy Themes and Thinkers, Cambridge University Press, 2005

- **POXON, B** - Religious Studies AS Philosophy, PushMe press, 2012

- **EYRE, C, KNIGHT, R, ROWE, G** - OCR Religious Studies Philosophy and Ethics A2, Heinemann, 2009

- **TAYLOR, M** - OCR Philosophy of Religion for AS and A2, Routledge, 2009

- **WILKINSON, M & CAMPBELL, H** - Philosophy of Religion for A2 Level, Continuum, 2009

Postscript

Brian Poxon was Head of Religious Studies at Wells Cathedral School until early 2014, and is an experienced examiner. He has taught at Bristol Cathedral School and Ballarat Grammar School, Australia, where he set up the successful Philosothon event for students. He is the author of several revision guides for PushMe Press.

Charlotte Davidson studied Theology at Durham University before completing her PGCE and starting work at Bolton School Girls' Division. She is now the Head of the Religious Studies Department at Cardinal Newman College in Preston, where she teaches Ethics and Philosophy of Religion and enjoys the challenge of engaging her students in debate about the big questions of morality and the existence of God.

Lightning Source UK Ltd.
Milton Keynes UK
UKOW05f1033031014

239563UK00002B/49/P